Too Dirty!

Written by Anne Rooney
Illustrated by Fabiano Fiorin

WAYLAND

Henry put on his
favourite jumper.

"You can't wear that,"
said Mum. "It's too dirty."
So Henry took it off.

Then Henry went into the kitchen to get a biscuit. He dropped his biscuit and it fell on the floor.

"You can't eat that now," said his sister, Kate. "It's too dirty."

Henry went into the garden
to play. He found a worm in
the mud.

SPLASH!

"Oops!" said Henry.

Henry and Axel walked
into the kitchen. They were
covered in mud.

"You can't come in here," shouted Mum. "You're too dirty!"

Henry took off his wellies and went upstairs.

He was very cross. Everyone just kept shouting at him.

In the bedroom, Kate was playing with his train set.

"Yuck! You're too dirty to play!" said Kate. "Go and have a bath."

"I don't like baths!" shouted Henry.

Henry went to the living room.

"Henry, you're too dirty to be in here," said Dad. "Go and have a bath, please."

Henry stomped off to the
bathroom in a bad mood.

Mum ran the water and told
Henry to get in.

"I don't want to," said Henry.

"Just get in the bath, Henry," said Mum.

Henry was very cross.
He climbed into the bath.

Axel looked around the
bathroom door.

"Out!" shouted Mum.

Suddenly, Axel jumped into
the bath, too.

"Oh, no!" shouted Henry.

There was dirty water everywhere! It went all over the walls.

It went all over the floor...

...and all over Mum!

"Mum, now you're TOO
DIRTY!" laughed Henry.

31

START READING is a series of highly enjoyable books for beginner readers. **The books have been carefully graded to match the Book Bands widely used in schools.** This enables readers to be sure they choose books that match their own reading ability.

Look out for the Band colour on the book in our Start Reading logo.

The Bands are:

Pink Band 1
Red Band 2
Yellow Band 3
Blue Band 4
Green Band 5
Orange Band 6
Turquoise Band 7
Purple Band 8
Gold Band 9

START READING books can be read independently or shared with an adult. They promote the enjoyment of reading through satisfying stories supported by fun illustrations.

Anne Rooney is often too dirty, but is too big to get told off for it. She lives in a state of chaos with her two daughters, a tortoise called Tor2 and a blue lobster called Marcel.

Fabiano Fiorin lives and works in a magical city, Venice, where there are canals full of sea water instead of roads, and there are boats instead of cars. Fabiano thinks the best thing about being an illustrator is that you can pretend to be the characters you draw and you can have lots of adventures.